D0122113

The Quotable Traveler

The Quotable Traveler

WISE WORDS FOR TRAVELERS, EXPLORERS, AND WANDERERS

RUNNING PRESS
PHILADELPHIA • LONDON

A Running Press Miniature Edition™

Copyright © 1994 by Running Press. Printed in Singapore.
All rights reserved under the Pan-American and International
Copyright Conventions.

Canadian representatives: General Publishing Co., Ltd.,
30 Lesmill Road, Don Mills, Ontario M3B 2T6. International
representatives: Worldwide Media Services, Inc.,
30 Montgomery Street, Jersey City, New Jersey 07302.
Library of Congress Cataloging-in-Publication Number 93-85532
ISBN 1-56138-361-9
This book may be ordered by mail from the publisher.
Please include $1.00 for postage and handling.
But try your bookstore first!
Running Press Book Publishers
125 South Twenty-second Street
Philadelphia, Pennsylvania 19103-4399

Contents

INTRODUCTION 7

TRAVELER'S ADVISORY 11

ON DEPARTURE 29

EN ROUTE 43

BEING THERE 69

COMING HOME 105

Introduction

Some journeys take us
away from it all, to places
no one knows us; some
take us to where it seems
we've always been. But
whether we venture to a

new part of town or into
an entirely new culture,
travel forever changes the
boundaries of the world
we once knew.

Here are the insights
of well-known travelers,
from Mark Twain to Anne
Tyler. These opinions and
advice about going there,
being there, and coming

home remind us that at
the end of the journey—
wherever we've been—
what matters is the
journey itself.

Traveler's Advisory

. . . all any of us need is a
very light suitcase.

—OSWALD WYND
B. 1913
SCOTTISH WRITER

Keep moving.

—HUNTER S. THOMPSON
B. 1939
AMERICAN WRITER

A good traveler is one
who does not know where
he is going to, and a perfect traveler does not
know where he came
from.

—LIN YUTANG
(1895–1976)
CHINESE WRITER

If you come to a fork in
the road, take it.

—YOGI BERRA
20TH-CENTURY AMERICAN ATHLETE

How much a dunce that
    has been sent to roam
Excels a dunce that has
    been kept at home.

—WILLIAM COWPER
(1731–1800)
ENGLISH POET

I always take abroad with me one really good soft pillow—to me it makes all the difference between comfort and misery.

—AGATHA CHRISTIE
(1891–1975)
ENGLISH WRITER

He that is a traveller must
have the back of an ass to
bear all, a tongue like the
tail of a dog to flatter all,
the mouth of a hog to eat
what is set before him, the
ear of a merchant to hear
all and say nothing . . .

—THOMAS NASHE
(1567–1601)
ENGLISH WRITER

To be sure that your
    friend is a friend,
You must go with him on
    a journey,
Travel with him day
    and night,
Go with him near and far.

—ANGOLAN PROVERB

Even disasters—there are always disasters when you travel—can be turned into adventures.

—MARILYN FRENCH
B. 1929
AMERICAN WRITER

The journey not the
arrival matters.

—T. S. ELIOT
(1888–1965)
AMERICAN-BORN BRITISH POET

Better far off to leave half
the ruins and nine-tenths
of the churches unseen
and to see well the rest; to
see them not once, but
again and often again; to

watch them, to learn
them, to live with them,
to love them, till they
have become a part of life
and life's recollections.

—AUGUSTUS HARE
19TH-CENTURY ENGLISH WRITER

I believe I have a sunny
disposition, and am not
naturally a grouch. It
takes a lot of optimism,
after all, to be a traveler.

—PAUL THEROUX
B. 1941
AMERICAN WRITER

Don't panic.

—DOUGLAS ADAMS
B. 1952
ENGLISH WRITER

On Departure

Venice 2341

Most people have that fantasy of catching the train that whistles in the night.

—WILLIE NELSON
B. 1933
AMERICAN SINGER

... the open road is a beckoning, a strangeness, a place where a man can lose himself.

—WILLIAM LEAST HEAT MOON
20TH-CENTURY AMERICAN WRITER

. . . I am going away with him to an unknown country where I shall have no past and no name, and where I shall be born again with a new face and an untried heart.

—COLETTE
(1873–1954)
FRENCH WRITER

A journey is a person in itself; no two are alike.

—JOHN STEINBECK
(1902–1968)
AMERICAN WRITER

. . . I travel not to go any-
where, but to go. I travel
for travel's sake. The great
affair is to move.

—ROBERT LOUIS STEVENSON
(1850–1894)
SCOTTISH WRITER

So they take off after each
other straight into an end-
less black prairie. The sun
is just comin' down and
they can feel night on
their backs. . . . And they
keep ridin' like that
straight into the night.
And the one who's chasin'
doesn't know where the
other one is taking him.

And the one who's being chased doesn't know where he's going.

—SAM SHEPARD
B. 1943
AMERICAN PLAYWRIGHT

There are pioneer souls
    that blaze their paths
Where highways never
    ran.

—SAM WALTER FOSS
    (1858–1911)
    AMERICAN WRITER

A border is always a temptation.

—LARRY MCMURTRY
B. 1936
AMERICAN WRITER

. . . people don't take trips—trips take people.

—JOHN STEINBECK
(1902–1968)
AMERICAN WRITER

The journey of a thousand miles begins with one step.

—LAO TZU
(570–490 B.C.)
CHINESE PHILOSOPHER

En Route

Going up that river was like travelling back to the earliest beginnings of the world, when vegetation rioted on the earth and the big trees were kings. An empty stream, a great silence, an impenetrable forest. . . . The broadening waters flowed through a mob of wooded islands;

you lost your way on that
river as you would in a
desert, and butted all day
long against shoals, trying
to find the channel, till
you thought yourself
bewitched and cut off for
ever from everything you
had known once—some-
where—far away—in
another existence

perhaps. . . . I got used to
it afterwards.

—JOSEPH CONRAD
(1857–1924)
RUSSIAN-BORN ENGLISH WRITER

I might be going to hell in a bucket, but at least I'm enjoying the ride.

—BOB WEIR
20TH-CENTURY AMERICAN
SONGWRITER

Okay. You are somewhere, at least in theory, between Butte and Mobile, going faster than sound in a long metal container that is not in physical contact with anything. A slight jiggling sensation at your prostate (if you have one) is, essentially, all that is holding you up 30,000 feet above

something that looks like
a badly distressed suede
jacket but is in fact the
surface of the earth. You
have been served a brown
puddle with a lump in it, a
rectangle of pale-yellow
congealment, and some
kind of mineral-based
salad. There is a
wheeeeengneeeenngn

noise. The jiggle-at-the-
prostate feeling gives way
to a kind of giving-way
sensation. You are swal-
lowed by a cloud.

Rule one: Maintain
perspective.

—ROY BLOUNT, JR.
B. 1941
AMERICAN WRITER

There are only two
emotions in a plane:
boredom and terror.

—*ORSON WELLES*
(1915–1985)
AMERICAN ACTOR

The stride of passengers
off an airplane is
always jauntier than the
stride on.

—TOM CLANCY
B. 1947
AMERICAN WRITER

I have never had any idea
what goes on with other
people—but I have found
that my major concern in
traveling in foreign parts
is where is the ladies'
room. Now, in an airplane
it always seems that it is
as far away from me as
possible. And that the
more complicated and

embarrassing the trip, the
more frequent my desire
to make it.

—KATHARINE HEPBURN
B. 1909
AMERICAN WRITER

What is the feeling when
you're driving away from
people and they recede on
the plane till you see their
specks dispersing?

—JACK KEROUAC
(1922–1969)
AMERICAN WRITER

Road food is always
neutral in color and taste.
It only turns exciting a
couple of hours later.

—THOMAS COBB
B. 1947
AMERICAN WRITER

I have never been one for life on the ocean wave. To begin with, I don't understand the theory of *mal de mer*, or seasickness, as it is euphemistically called in our country. What causes it? Is it some dislocation in the inner ear? Does the retching come from fried

foods and unripe water-
melon balls?

—GROUCHO MARX
(1890–1977)
AMERICAN COMEDIAN

Hitchhiking is not a sport. It is not an art. It certainly isn't work, for it requires no particular ability nor does it produce anything of value. It's an adventure, I suppose,

but a shallow, ignoble
adventure. Hitchhiking is
parasitic, no more than a
reckless panhandling, as
far as I can see.

—TOM ROBBINS
B. 1936
AMERICAN WRITER

Hitchhiking is a cumulative experience, a never-ending happening of unknown factors which contribute, with a little luck, to a memory of what real travelling is all about —not just the chance to say that you've been to a place, but the feeling that at one time, somewhere,

even if only for an instant,
you felt like you had
become a part of the land
through which you
travelled.

—KEN WELSH
B. 1941
AMERICAN WRITER

So the Hieronymus Bosch
bus headed out of Kesey's
place with the destination
sign in front reading
"Further" and a sign in the
back saying "Caution:
Weird Load." It was
weird, all right, but it
was euphoria on board,
barreling through all that
warm California sun in

July, on the road, and everything they had been working on at Kesey's was on board and heading on Further.

—TOM WOLFE
B. 1930
AMERICAN WRITER

Your road is everything
that a road ought to be
. . . and yet you will not
stay in it half a mile, for
the reason that little,
seductive, mysterious
roads are always branching
out from it on either
hand, and as these curve
sharply also and hide what
is beyond, you cannot

resist the temptation to
desert your own chosen
road and explore them.

—MARK TWAIN
(1835–1910)
AMERICAN WRITER

Being There

To awaken quite alone in a strange town is one of the pleasantest sensations in the world.

—FREYA STARK
B. 1893
BRITISH WRITER

Your travel life has the essence of a dream. It is something outside the normal, yet you are in it. It is peopled with characters you have never seen before and in all probability will never see again. It brings occasional homesickness, and lone-liness, and pangs of

longing. . . . But you are like the Vikings or the master mariners of the Elizabethan age, who have gone into a world of adventure, and home is not home until you return.

—AGATHA CHRISTIE (1890–1976) ENGLISH WRITER

The use of travelling is to
regulate imagination by
reality, and instead of
thinking how things
may be, to see them as
they are.

—SAMUEL JOHNSON
(1696–1772)
AMERICAN PHILOSOPHER

Most travelers content
themselves with what they
may chance to see from
car-windows, hotel veran-
das, or the deck of a
steamer . . . clinging to
the battered highways like
drowning sailors to a
liferaft.

—JOHN MUIR
(1838–1914)
AMERICAN NATURALIST

A good traveler has no fixed plans and is not intent on arriving.

—LAO TZU
(570–490 B.C.)
CHINESE PHILOSOPHER

Too often . . . I would
hear men boast only of the
miles covered that day,
rarely of what they
had seen.

—LOUIS L'AMOUR
(1908–1988)
AMERICAN WRITER

When you are at sea you know you must reach harbor, to restock and hope, rest in a warm caress. You need ports and often can't wait to get to the next.

Then when you are in port, you can't wait to get back to the sea again. . . . You need mother earth, but you love the sea.

—STEVEN CALLAHAN
B. 1952
AMERICAN WRITER

I dislike feeling at home
when I am abroad.

—GEORGE BERNARD SHAW
(1856–1950)
ENGLISH WRITER

The treachery of the phrase book . . . is that you cannot begin to follow the answer to the question you've pronounced so beautifully—and, worse still, your auditor now assumes you're fluent in Swahili.

—PICO IYER
B. 1957
ENGLISH WRITER

How To Speak a
Foreign Language:
The key is to understand
that foreigners communi-
cate by means of
"idiomatic expressions,"
the main ones being:

GERMAN: "Ach du
lieber!" ("Darn it!")

SPANISH: "Caramba!"
("Darn it!")

FRENCH: "Zut alors!" ("Look! A lors!")

Also you should bear in mind that foreign persons for some reason believe that everyday household objects and vegetables are "masculine" and "feminine."

—DAVE BARRY
B. 1947
AMERICAN WRITER

I have wandered all my life, and I have also travelled; the difference between the two being this, that we wander for distraction, but we travel for fulfillment.

—*HILAIRE BELLOC*
(1870–1953)
FRENCH-BORN ENGLISH WRITER

This was the moment I
longed for every day.
Settling at a heavy
inn-table, thawing and
tingling, with wine, bread,
and cheese handy and my
papers, books and diary all
laid out; writing up the
day's doings, hunting for
words in the dictionary,

drawing, struggling with
verses, or merely subsiding
in a vacuous and content-
ed trance while the snow
thawed off my boots.

—PATRICK LEIGH FERMOR
B. 1915
BRITISH WRITER

. . . travel is more than the seeing of sights; it is a change that goes on, deep and permanent, in the ideas of living.

—MIRIAM BEARD
B. 1901
AMERICAN WRITER

The river delights to lift
us free, if only we dare to
let go. Our true work
is this voyage, this
adventure.

—RICHARD BACH
B. 1936
AMERICAN WRITER

A good holiday is one
spent among people whose
notions of time are vaguer
than yours.

—JOHN BOYNTON PRIESTLY
(1894–1984)
ENGLISH WRITER

The earth belongs to anyone who stops for a moment, gazes and goes on his way . . .

—COLETTE
(1873–1954)
FRENCH WRITER

The desert, like a powerful magnet, changes those who come within its field. Many travelers have felt it to be an almost mystical experience; others, a challenge to their humanity, to their very survivability. Some have found peace, some despair. Others have created from

inner resources monu-
ments of literature,
philosophy, and religion.
Perhaps the desert is no
more than a magnifying
lens, something that
enables man to write large
whatever he truly is.

—WILLIAM R. POLK AND
WILLIAM J. MARES
20TH-CENTURY
AMERICAN SCHOLARS

"The world is only
tolerable because of the
empty places in it—
millions of people all
crowded together, fighting
and struggling, but behind
them, somewhere, enor-
mous, empty places. I tell
you what I think," he said,
"when the world's filled
up, we'll have to get hold

of a star. Any star. Venus,
or Mars. Get hold of it
and leave it empty. Man
needs an empty space
somewhere for his spirit
to rest in."

—DORIS LESSING
B. 1919
BRITISH NOVELIST

Traveling carries with it
the curse of being at home
everywhere and yet
nowhere, for wherever one
is some part of oneself
remains on another
continent.

—MARGOT FONTEYN
(1919–1991)
ENGLISH BALLERINA

I think that maybe we
do not climb a mountain
because it is there.
We climb it because
we are here.

—JON CARROLL
20TH-CENTURY AMERICAN WRITER

The healthy wayfarer
sitting beside the road
scanning the horizon open
before him, is he not the
absolute master of the
earth, the waters, and
even the sky? What
housedweller can vie with
him in power and wealth?
His estate has no limits,
his empire no law. No

word bends him toward
the ground, for the bounty
and beauty of the world
are already his.

—*ISABELLE EBERHARDT*
B. 1933
AMERICAN WRITER

On a bicycle I am exposed to all local experiences as no other modern traveller can hope to be. Moving quietly along at gentle speeds allows me to see, hear, and smell the country, in a way which isn't possible encapsulated in a motorcar or a bus. I can stop wherever and when-

ever I want to, unlike the
motorized traveller, and
am able to respond to the
greetings of workers in the
fields, passers-by, and
friendly villagers.

—BETTINA SELBY
B. 1934
ENGLISH WRITER

It began in mystery, and it
will end in mystery, but
what a savage and
beautiful country lies
in between.

—DIANE ACKERMAN
B. 1948
AMERICAN WRITER

No matter where you go—
there you are.

—EARL MACRAUCH
20TH-CENTURY AMERICAN WRITER

Coming Home

Take only memories.
Leave nothing but
footprints.

—CHIEF SEATTLE
(1786–1866)
SUQUAMISH CHIEF

Looking back on a sojourn
in the African highlands,
you are struck by your
feeling of having lived for
a time up in the air.

—ISAK DINESEN
(1885–1962)
DANISH WRITER

The real voyage of discovery consists not in seeing new landscapes, but in having new eyes.

—MARCEL PROUST
(1871–1922)
FRENCH WRITER

All travel is circular. I had been jerked through Asia, making a parabola on one of the planet's hemispheres. After all, the grand tour is just the inspired man's way of heading home.

—PAUL THEROUX
B. 1941
AMERICAN WRITER

If an ass goes traveling,
he'll not come home
a horse.

—*Thomas Fuller*
(1608–1661)
English clergyman

How hard it is to escape
from places. However
carefully one goes they
hold you—you leave bits
of yourself fluttering on
the fences—little rags and
shreds of your very life.

—KATHERINE MANSFIELD
(1888–1923)
ENGLISH WRITER

. . . I hadn't had a perfect
moment yet, and I always
like to have one before I
leave an exotic place.
They're a good way of

bringing things to an end.
But you can never plan for
one. You never know when
they're coming. It's sort of
like falling in love . . .
with yourself.

—SPALDING GRAY
B. 1941
AMERICAN MONOLOGUIST

A man travels the world
over in search of what he
needs and returns home to
find it.

—*GEORGE MOORE*
(1852–1933)
IRISH NOVELIST

Now, when I have trouble
getting to sleep, I some-
times imagine that my bed
is on the back of a flatbed
pickup truck driving
across the Great Plains.
. . . The back of the truck
has sides but no top.
I can see the stars. The air
is cool. . . . The Great

Plains which I cross in my
sleep are bigger than any
name people give them.
They are enormous, boun-
tiful, unfenced, empty of
buildings, full of names
and stories. They extend
beyond the frame of the
photograph. Their hills
are hipped, like a woman

asleep under a sheet.
Their rivers rhyme.

—IAN FRAZIER
B. 1951
AMERICAN WRITER

. . . once you have trav-
eled, the voyage never
ends, but is played out
over and over again in the
quietest chambers . . . the
mind can never break off
from the journey.

—PAT CONROY
B. 1945
AMERICAN WRITER

. . . I think about all the different ways we leave people in this world. Cheerily waving goodbye to some at airports, knowing we'll never see each other again. Leaving others on the side of the road, hoping that we will.

—AMY TAN
B. 1952
AMERICAN WRITER

"Don't worry," he adds,
"it'll all still be here
next spring."

The sun goes down, I
face the road again, we
light up our after-dinner
cigars. Keeping the flame
alive. The car races
forward through a world
dissolving into snow
and night.

Yes, I agree that's a good thought and it better be so. Or by God there

might be trouble. The
desert will still be here in
the spring. And then
comes another thought.
When I return will it be
the same? Will I be the
same? Will anything ever
be quite the same again?
If I return.

—EDWARD ABBEY
(1927–1989)
AMERICAN WRITER

The road was new to me,
as roads always are,
going back.

—SARAH ORNE JEWETT
(1849–1909)
AMERICAN WRITER

Acknowledgements

The excerpt on pages 49–51 by Roy Blount, Jr. from *Now Where Were We?*, copyright © 1990 by Roy Blount, Jr., is reprinted by permission of Ballantine.

The excerpt on pages 82–83 by Dave Barry from *Dave Barry's Greatest Hits*, copyright © 1988 by Dave Barry, is reprinted by permission of Crown Publishers, Inc. and the Fox Chase Agency.